GW00733379

SPRINGS OF LIVING WATER

John Lochran

Springs of Living Water

REFLECTIONS ON
THE MESSAGE OF LOURDES

THE COLUMBA PRESS
DUBLIN

First edition, 1996, published by
THE COLUMBA PRESS
55A Spruce Avenue, Stillorgan Industrial Park,
Blackrock, Co Dublin, Ireland

Cover by Bill Bolger
Illustrations by Virginie Cuvelier, Boulogne-sur-Mer
Origination by The Columba Press
Printed in Ireland by Genprint Ltd, Dublin

ISBN 1 85607 163 4

Contents

Introduction

On May 12 1866, just a few weeks before leaving Lourdes to enter the convent of Nevers in the north of France, Bernadette wrote an account of the apparitions entitled *'Journal dedié à la Reine du Ciel'* (Journal dedicated to the Queen of Heaven). It was one of the rare occasions when Bernadette referred to Our Lady as Queen. Even the title *'Immaculate Conception'*, a title revealed to Bernadette by Our Lady herself, was seldom used. Throughout her religious life she preferred the more intimate and familiar expression *'Oh Mary my mother'*.

In doing so Bernadette makes no attempt to deny the Queenship of Mary. On the contrary, she points us to where the real essence of Mary's royalty lies: not in the grandeur, opulence and pride that characterize the superpowers of this world, but in the greatness of a tender maternal love born of God and lived with God. Our Lady is *'more a Mother than a Queen'* said Thérèse of

Lisieux. For Bernadette there is no 'more' or 'less'. Being Queen and Mother are just different ways of expressing the one unique reality of the woman *'full of grace'*. The regal power of Mary finds its highest expression in the humble maternal service of love.

In revealing herself to Bernadette as the 'Immaculate Conception' Mary reveals more than her priviledged position before God. Above all she tells us that the purest of creatures has not abandoned her children; that the woman conceived without sin never abandons the sinner. Many accounts of the apparitions have Mary revealing her identity to Bernadette while remaining high up in the recess of the rock known as Massabielle. Original accounts state otherwise. Mary in fact descended from the rock. She came down to the little visionary. In the words of Bernadette herself 'she was so close I could almost touch her'. Here is the very image of the incarnation itself, the image of Jesus who came down from heaven to draw close to us, to enfold the whole of humanity in the embrace of his divine love. In drawing close to Bernadette, Mary reveals again the nearness of God, the gift of divine love offered to all in Jesus. To each and to everyone is offered a share in her 'fullness of grace', no matter the state of our hearts. Here is the Queen longing for us to be part of the heavenly kingdom. Here is the mother longing to enfold all her children within the mantle of her love, and especially those who have wandered far from home.

Massabielle, before and during the apparitions, was both the local town rubbish dump and a pig-sty. If anyone in the town of Lourdes behaved badly the locals would say: *'They must have been brought up at Massabielle'*. It is to such a place, a place associated with the riff-raff, the low life of the times, that Mary comes. In doing so, Our Lady affirms the presence of an often ugly world, often peopled by ugly hearts. But more importantly, she reminds us that Jesus came 'to seek out and save what was lost'. We do not need to deny the reality of evil either within us or around us. Mary invites us to face it and to transform it. We can break free from our dark ways and grow to the royal stature of true sons and daughters of a heavenly Father. With the apparitions, being 'brought up at Massabielle' takes on new meaning. Our 'low life' can be transformed into divine life.

A few weeks before leaving Lourdes, as my term of office as Chaplain for the English-speaking pilgrims was coming to a close, I decided to begin these reflections. Like Bernadette, I too wished to write a few thoughts dedicated to the Queen of heaven. I dedicate them to Our Lady of Lourdes and to you, the pilgrim, who will read and ponder them. I pray they may lead you to a greater discovery and knowledge of the Queen who is our Mother. She waits for you here in Lourdes. She waits for each of us on whatever particular road we may travel, to guide us onwards on our journey of faith. Here at Massabielle, and on the roads where we live, Mary wants 'to bring us up' the 'right way'. This is the 'pilgrim way' she herself travelled on the road before us as she walked with Jesus through all the events of his life towards deeper intimacy with the heavenly Father. Her royal maternal embrace is always there for us, to lead us in the only way that can transform our lives, the way of Jesus, the way of a divine and royal humanity. She waits for us here in Lourdes to make us attentive to the presence of Jesus and to what he offers us: *springs of living water*.

1. Every picture tells a story

Most of us, at some point of our lives, have gone to visit a museum or art gallery. Some are very famous places like the British Museum in London or the Louvre in Paris. In these places precious objects and famous paintings abound. Every picture tells a story, so the saying goes, and generally the saying is true. Every picture does tell a story; a story of the times in which the painting was made, the social conditions, the political atmosphere, the concerns and problems of the era. Portraits tell the story of the people they depict; their fame or notoriety, their history and background. Every picture tells a story and these masterpieces and works of art do just that.

However there is one portrait you will not find in these famous places – a very simple portrait – the portrait of Bernadette Soubirous. In the art world it will never be considered a masterpiece, but for those of us acquainted with Lourdes this simple little portrait tells a story much deeper and greater than most of the masterpieces of the world put together.

'The lamp of the body is the eye. It follows that if the eye is sound, the whole body will be filled with light.' These are the words of Jesus in the Gospels. He speaks of the physical but points to the spiritual. Do we live in light or do we live in darkness? When you look at the simple portrait of Bernadette, you are struck by her eyes. You begin to realize what Jesus means. Her eyes are full of light, not the light that just comes from physically seeing, but a deeper light, an inner light. *'Where your treasure is, there is your heart also.'* When we look at the eyes of this 14-year-old child, we know where her treasure is. Her eyes tell us she has seen something of heaven here on earth.

In *Forgotten among the Lilies*, Ronald Rolheiser remarks that much time is spent looking at ourselves in the mirror: 'we sometimes scrutinize and examine ourselves. We see the signs of ageing; the bags under our eyes, more grey hair … We all do that. What we need to do is to look ourselves straight in the eyes and see what they tell us. Are they tired, cynical, lifeless?' I agree with Rolheiser. Growing old for a Christian is more about the spirit than it is about the body. We

need to recover our sparkle. That's
Gospels are about. Not to live in darkn
light, not to grow old through the pres
illusions of the world but to grow young again in
the spirit of God. We need to recover the light in
our spirit.

You may remember Marilyn Monroe, the
famous American actress of the 50s and 60s. In a
song called 'Candle in the Wind', Elton John, the
singer, spoke about Marilyn Monroe:

So it seems to me you lived your life like a Candle in the
*   Wind*
never knowing who to cling to when the rains came in.
I would have liked to know you, but I was just a kid.
The candle burned out long before the legend ever did.

This was a good description of Marilyn Monroe's
life. She was just like that, a 'candle in the wind'.
She never knew who to cling to. Many of the
people around her were more interested in their
own ambitions and advantages than in her wel-
fare. This woman had great difficulty in finding
a safe embrace. So the candle burned out. Her
life ended, snuffed out in tragic circumstances.
The flame was already beginning to wane long
before her physical death. I imagine that she

.en found herself in darkness, engulfed by the dark currents around her.

The words of the song were written for Marilyn Monroe but they can apply to each of us. We are all something of the 'candle in the wind'. The candle is a symbol for each one of us. The light we have as children of God can be easily snuffed out by the darkness of the world around us. This happens when we cling to what is false, to wrong values, to the wrong people. It happens when our ego, the great 'I am' replaces the Lord who is. It happens when we cling to the illusory happiness offered by the world. It happens when we prefer to remain blind to the ways of God.

There is an account in Mark's Gospel of Jesus healing a blind man:

'He took the blind man by the hand and led him outside the village. Then putting spittle on his eyes and laying his hands on him, he asked: 'Can you see anything?' The man who was beginning to see, replied: 'I can see people; they look like trees to me, but they are walking about.' Then he laid his hands on the man again and he saw clearly.' (Mk. 8:22-26)

Jesus led the man 'outside the village'. Jesus has

to take him far from his secure world, his familiar ways, to bring about a healing encounter. It is precisely within this context that we need to hear again Our Lady's invitation to *'come here on pilgrimage'*. The word 'pilgrimage' as used by Mary in the local dialect of Bernadette's time means exactly this: to move 'outside our own secure, familiar place to meet with others'. Mary does not just mean 'pilgrimage' as moving from one place to another place. It is above all an invitation to meet not just 'others' but 'Another'. To follow a deeper movement of the spirit, leaving behind our old usual ways of thinking and acting to come to a personal healing encounter with the Lord. For Jesus himself, his own death and resurrection happened *'outside the city'*, outside Jerusalem. Both the Gospel message and the message of Lourdes point us in the same direction. We are given a call to quit the familiar and often stagnant paths we follow, to die to the often sinful world we know, the world of illusions and false values, and rise to new life. Our Lady wishes that we leave the ways of our own inner blindness and discover a new vision of life and of love.

In the Gospel story, the blind man was led by the hand. Jesus takes him by the hand. We cannot ourselves. We cannot bring change about by ourselves. We need another to guide us. Mary never points to herself. She always points to her son. *'Do whatever he tells you,'* she said at Cana. She continues to repeat the same message. We need Another to lead, to guide us, to enable us to see. *'Whoever follows me will not walk in darkness, he will have the light of life.'* The blind man begins to see again, but not instantly. His was a gradual, progressive healing. If we follow Jesus who is the Light of the world, if we commit our lives to his word, then little by little we will recover the sparkle in our hearts. Perhaps our hearts are heavy with many concerns, perhaps broken, perhaps lost. Perhaps there are circumstances that are seemingly impossible to resolve. We need not lose heart. We just need to hold out our hand for another to take. He will take it. He knows that it is our whole being that needs to be healed. If we allow ourselves to be led by the hand of God, all that is heavy in our lives, all that prevents us from following the ways of his kingdom, will disappear. Little by little the light will come. Gradually the Lord will possess our hearts and transform our circumstances. It is only the vision of his love and the power of his mercy that can give us the courage to see again, to look at the truth, to face what we need to face. All healing, physical as well as spiritual is given to us so that we may grow under the working of his grace.

Today our eye sees further and our horizons have become wider. The means of knowledge and communication have never been greater. With the highly sophisticated technology we possess, we can explore the wonders of the infinitely small and the infinitely great. Nothing happens on the planet that cannot be communicated almost immediately. But knowing is not necessarily seeing.

For *to see*, according to the message of Jesus, is to go beyond the appearances, to go beyond the surface. It is to discover what lies hidden at the heart of people and events. It is to look at the visible and see the invisible that surrounds it and sustains it.

To see is to be born anew to the beauty of the world; to contemplate the splendours of the universe, to wonder at the astonishing gifts that people possess.

To see is to discover that God is not remote, absent from the affairs of the world. He is at work among us. He is with us always.

To see is to discover the greatness of God's love for us. 'I looked at her all I could,' said Bernadette. In beholding, in keeping our eyes on the Lord we discover what love is, and love, as Shakespeare said, *'adds a precious seeing to the eye...'*

This discovery is never spontaneous. It demands that we allow another to remove the scales from our eyes, to free us from our blindness, to lead us by the hand out of our darkness into the light of new vision and life. *'O Jesus, enlighten the inner eyes of my heart,'* Bernadette said. As we look at the simple portrait of Bernadette, we see how much his light shines. Yes, every picture tells a story.

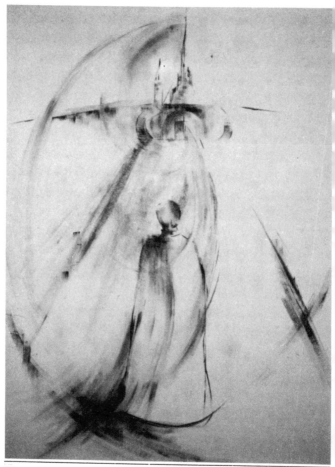

2. Travelling Light

The pilgrimage beckons. We're about to set off on a journey. It's time to pack our bags and get going. It's time to say goodbye. To what? To all and to nothing. To nothing for the kind of familiar world we leave will always be there, close to us, around us, in us. To all, for the journey is not like any other we have made before. It is a journey in search of God, in search of the divine. Travel as lightly as possible. Excess baggage on a journey like this can be a drawback. That means we have to abandon whatever might hinder the journey, whatever might impede the divine action within us and deflect us from reaching our destination.

Saying goodbye can be a painful experience. It's not easy to say goodbye to the ones we love. For a pilgrim it can even be harder. For the one we need to say goodbye to most of all is our very own self. It's a goodbye to that spirit of independence and self-seeking that desires to go its own way and quickly wanders from the divine path It's a goodbye to the hurly burly of our noisy existence. We need to say farewell to frenzy, to agitation, to the myriad of voices that invade us. How else will we be able to hear the voice of God speak to the depths of our hearts? It's a goodbye to familiar patterns of life, familiar habits, to recognizable landmarks. For we are about to enter unknown territory. *'Go from your country and your kindred and your father's house to the land that I will show you.'* (Gen 12:1)

Faith demands that we leave our familiar world, however comfortable it may be, and go in search of the promised land of God's love. The experienced traveller knows what to take and what to leave behind. Experience is a great teacher. But we are not always experienced travellers. Mostly we take too much or too little. But this is no ordinary journey. Little by little as we advance on our way we will see what we have to discard. The essential is to set out with a self that's not turned inward but outward, for God is the Other that we are going to meet. In that sense we need to travel light.

Travelling light means we don't have to meet God wearing our 'Sunday Best' as some pilgrims seem to think. You can recognize them immediately. They've dressed themselves up in pious airs and saintly smiles. Wanting to enter the spirit of things, they don another character, another personality. We dress for the occasion and end up as a shadow of our real selves. And so a kind of saint disembarks with an artificial glow that you know will never last. Before God we don't need to pretend. We just need to bring before him the real and the essential. We come just as we are. That is the real and the essential. We need to bring our body, our spirit, our good and our bad, our sinful past and present, our hopes and fears, our inclinations whether good or evil … everything that is truly ourselves. God wishes to have a real being before him; one who knows how to laugh and to cry; one who knows the price of human love and the attraction of the sexes; one who can turn to him and one who can even resist him. With God, honesty is always the best policy.

Remember we don't have to climb a mountain to reach the Lord. He comes to us. That's what the Incarnation means. The Blessed Virgin descended from the rock to draw close to Bernadette. Jesus descended from heaven to draw close to us.

Travel light: *'Take nothing for your journey, no staff nor bag, nor bread, nor money…'* (Lk 9:2) He is not drawn to us with all our riches and possessions. We don't have to clothe ourselves to hide our nakedness. We can stand before him in all our poverty, in all our lostness. Humility, poverty littleness are the only passports we need. They will lead us out of the frontiers of self to meet the Other who waits to meet us.

Travel Light. If we take on board everyone else's experiences we will never make our own. There's always someone who wants to tell us about the wonderful feelings they've had, the great sensations they've felt praying in front of the Grotto. Maybe something special did come their way. All the better. But if we find emptiness and not ecstasy, if we find dryness instead of elation, we must not feel that there is something wrong with us. We are all unique. God speaks to each of us in different ways. Feelings can easily come with the euphoria of the occasion. Faith is made of sterner stuff: *'Blessed are those who do not see and yet believe.'* If we are here it is because the Lord led us to be here. He will not let us leave without some 'souvenir'. We will not go home empty handed.

There will be guides on the journey. They come

in all shapes and forms. Some will be helpful and may enable us to live this moment in a fruitful way. Others will just be happy to fill up our time. As long as we're doing all that duty requires, and following some kind of pious and devotional practices, they will consider it a job done, even if not all that well done. Such guides are not a help. They only serve to stifle the creative power of God's love. Since the end of our journey is God, no one knows the way except the one who comes from God, that is Jesus. While we can listen to the guides, we need to keep our eyes fixed firmly on him for he is *the Way, the Truth and the Life.* He is the road that Abraham takes in leaving his country towards the promised land. He is the pillar of cloud and fire that shows the way forward to the Israelites in the desert. He is the road that leads all men to the Father. We have to follow him – there is no other way. He is the truth that humankind has searched for throughout the ages. What philosophers, thinkers, the learned and the holy men of every religion have glimpsed as truth becomes complete in him. It is Jesus who gives meaning and value to all things. Most importantly, he is life. He is the life that we search for and which often eludes us. He is the life of the spirit, of the body, human and divine life, eternal life. He is the life that only he, who was raised by the Father, can give. When we are on the road with him we know where we are going, we know we are living in the truth, we know we have a life that no one can take away. Just as he met the disciples on the roads where they walked and lived, just as he met the peoples by the lake and in the valleys, so he waits to meet us as we pass by. *'Have people come in pilgrimage,'* Our Lady said to Bernadette. And we have come, come to *'drink at the source'*, come to be refreshed in his love and there to find again our purpose, the meaning of our Christian lives.

'In heaven I will forget no one,' Bernadette said. She will be on the journey with us. *'The Grotto was my heaven on earth,'* she said. As we travel with her on our way, she will not forget us. She will be praying to Mary and Jesus that we too arrive at our destination and taste, here in this sacred place, something of that heaven, something of that love that she herself experienced. Travel light and you will travel far!

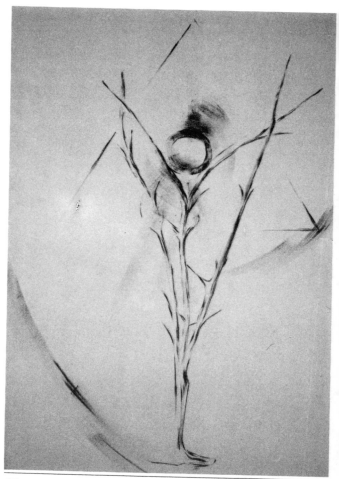

3. Food for the Journey

We find it hard to identify with the saints. They are not like the rest of us. They seem to carry within themselves some kind of immunity from the problems that we lesser mortals are subject to. We think they are given some special grace that makes life easier, more transparent, more manageable. Into that category we place Bernadette. Graced with visions, she had it made. That's how we feel. Her life is steeped in much romantic hype. Everything that happens to her happens in a warm glow. She sails through life on the waves of a constant God-filled ecstasy.

This is not the real Bernadette. Bernadette was very much part of the real world. Her sickness, her pain, her suffering were real. In Bernadette we touch the wounds. Before the apparitions she was sick, starving and destitute. During the apparitions she was laughed at, misunderstood, opposed and threatened. After the apparitions it doesn't get any easier. Six years after the apparitions, Bernadette left Lourdes to become a nun in the convent of Nevers in the north of France. It must have been one of the most painful moments of her life. Lourdes was a place that meant everything to her. The place where she had grown up. The place that meant home and family. The place that would always mean the apparitions. *'The Grotto was my heaven'*, she said. Now she has to leave this particular heaven and never return. She has to leave this heaven and embrace another life, another world, another reality.

The journey Bernadette makes is much more than the physical movement from one geographical location to another. It is more than just going from Lourdes to Nevers. She is being asked by God to undertake a journey of faith, to let go of the familiar faces and places. She is to set out on an unknown path, to unknown places, to unknown faces. Bernadette leaves all that is familiar. She enters an unknown, and even at times, hostile environment. The convent was no bed of roses. Bernadette did not have an easy journey through life. Yes she saw something of heaven, but afterwards she had to live like the rest of us in the obscurity of faith. Yes she had her moments of ecstasy, but only moments. Constant ecstasy is for paradise alone and Bernadette did not live in paradise. She had to live out her life in the real world, with all its pains and problems, questions and complexities.

With Bernadette we begin to grasp something of the journey of faith that God asks each of us to make through life. New situations arise that can easily turn our familiar world upside down: sudden and serious sickness, the sudden death of a loved one or friend, a marriage break up, a move to a new job or town, the painful prospect or reality of retirement, and so on. Many factors enter our lives and cause crisis. We don't always see the how or the why. We don't know where we are going. Suddenly nothing is familiar. We find ourselves with nothing to hold on to, adrift in unknown and often hostile territory. At such times our anguish can be great. We cling to fear, anxiety, discouragement, despair or anger. Bernadette points to another way of living these circumstances. Not against God but with God. She decides to make the journey with God, to live the questions, the fears and the anguish with him. She knows God provides food for the journey.

At a troubled moment in Israel's history, we find the prophet Elijah fleeing for his life and taking refuge in the wilderness. Harassed, hounded and humiliated he just wants to lie down and die. An angel of the Lord appears to him saying: *'Get up and eat, otherwise the journey will be too much for you.'* (1 Kings 19:7) Nourished and strengthened Elijah is able to continue his journey and meet God on the mountain of Horeb.

In the troubled times of our existence, when everything feels too much for us, Jesus doesn't want us to lie down and die. He has a food to give us; a food that will strengthen us and give us the energy to make the further inner journey that leads to life. Like Elijah before him, Jesus goes into the wilderness. After forty days and nights of fasting, he is hungry. This time it is Satan who disrupts the journey. He tempts Jesus: *'If you are the Son of God change these stones into bread.'* (Mt 4:3) We know that Jesus will eventually multiply loaves for the multitude following him. But he does not do this for himself. Instead he replies, *'One does not live on bread alone, but on every word that comes from the mouth of God.'* (Mt 4:4) Jesus reveals the importance of the word of God. This is the food he wants us to have. This is 'the power of God to build us up'.

The word of Scripture is not some dead record or

memory of the past. It is a living word addres
to each of us personally in the here and now
our everyday existence. When Jesus spoke he
was thinking not just of the people of his own
time but of every time. When Jesus spoke he was
thinking about us ... he speaks and the blind see,
the deaf hear and the lame walk ... he speaks
and his word heals the sick and the sinner ... he
speaks and the course of life is changed, the
stone rolls away from the tomb and the dead rise
again ... his word gives life to saddened hearts,
troubled spirits and lonely souls. His word is for
each of us to bring calm to our anxious storms
and light to our darkened hearts. Our job is to listen. Our job is to satisfy our hungry and needy
hearts. Our job is to feed on the word held out to
us. This is the first food Jesus offers.

The second is revealed to the people that followed him all day and who had been fed the
evening before with miraculous bread. Now
Jesus goes beyond the physical to point to the
more deeply spiritual. He leads the multitude to
realize that he alone can satisfy all the hungers of
the heart. In the Gospel of John, Jesus reveals
himself as the Bread of Life given by the Father
to humanity. Jesus is the food of the Eucharist.

He is the 'living bread'; no abstract God who is far from us, but one who gives us what is vital, his own life.

Sometimes we complain that the Mass is boring. Maybe the priest who celebrates the Eucharist is boring, but never the Eucharist itself. As priests, it is for us to find words that relate the Christian message in a meaningful and relevant way. It is for us to ensure that our celebrations enliven and do not deaden our faith. But, at the same time, we are not at Mass to be entertained. We celebrate the Eucharist to be embraced. Jesus promised to be with us until the end of time. (Mt 28:20) The Eucharist is the reality of the promise; it is the reality of the eternal alliance, the never-ending embrace of God for humankind. That embrace, that alliance is not something we simply receive; it is something we share. We say that we 'receive' communion. The term is badly chosen. It implies passivity, that we are on the receiving end of something. The Eucharist is not merely about receiving; it is above all about giving. 'Do this in memory of me', is a call to share in the embrace of God's love, and a command to actively commit ourselves, to personally pledge ourselves to the work of love. A deeper union with the one who is the Bread of Life will nourish and enrich our love.

Jesus reveals a third nourishment. It happens in the presence of the apostles after the meeting with the Samaritan woman. While Jesus spoke with the Samaritan, the apostles went off in search of food. When they returned to the scene Jesus seemed to have lost all interest in eating. He was tired. Now they found him refreshed. He was different. He was joyful. And when they offered him food he replied: *'My food is to do the will of him who sent me.'* (Jn 4:34) It is the will of the Father that encompasses everything. It is the source and goal of the other foods. And it is in doing the will of the Father that we find life. His will is no barren affair but the loving desire of his heart for our lives. The word of God, the Eucharist, the will of the Father: this is the food that God provides for our journey.

'Father, I am not asking you to remove them from the world ... but to protect them from the evil one.' (Jn 17) Yes, we live in the real world, as Bernadette did. Jesus knows it well. He knows the dark forces that exist to disrupt our life and our journey towards his love and his peace. The evil one wants to make us sickly emaciated beings, people who

are underdeveloped. He wants to turn us into dwarfs. This is what the evil one wants for us at the spiritual level. He wants to inhibit the growth of the spiritual life by making sure we lack the three forms of food that Jesus wants to give.

The daughter of a miller, familiar with the making of bread, Bernadette knew the necessity of bread for life. As a child of God, she knew the necessity of another more important bread that comes from heaven. *'Give me the bread of seeing you in all things and at all times,'* she prayed. And the Lord gave her that bread. He gave her the daily bread she needed, not just to survive the difficult times, not just to put up with things, but the daily bread of his word and his presence that makes life the precious gift that it is. *'Get up and eat, otherwise the journey will be too much for you.'* (1 Kings 19:7) To be strong, to fight, to endure, to continue, we must eat.

O Jesus, give me
the bread of humility,
the bread of obedience,
the bread of charity,
the bread of melting my will to yours,
the bread of patience in suffering,
the bread of seeing you in all things and at all times.

(St Bernadette)

4. Waiting at the Well

Every pilgrimage is a journey in faith towards God. As the pilgrim seriously embarks on this journey he moves 'outside' his own familiar world towards a wider horizon. Some five million pilgrims do so every year as they make their way to the Grotto of Massabielle. They come from every corner of the globe and from all walks of life. In Lourdes vast international crowds are a daily reality. With so many people around, the lone pilgrim can easily feel swallowed up by the crowd. Am I just another person among the many, another face in the crowd, just another anonymous nobody? It's easy to feel that way. Yet each person is a world in himself, a world of ups and downs, hopes and fears, joys and sorrows. We all have our own personal story to tell and we come here to tell it. We come here to lay before the hearts of Mary and Jesus all our cares and concerns. But in the telling of our story a surprise awaits us. In telling our story we dis-

her story. This is the most personal
. a story God has to tell each of us, a
y the prophets and revealed in Jesus.
ry of God's love for us. Before his
heart, in his eyes, we are never anonymous,
never just another face in the crowd. We are the
chosen of God, *'blessed in Christ with every spiritual
blessing ...'* (Eph 1:3) As we come to tell our story,
we find God waiting for us with another story,
one that embraces the entire meaning of our own.

*'Near restful waters he leads me to revive my droop-
ing spirit.'* (Psalm 22) Our Lady echoes the words
of the psalm as she tells Bernadette and each of
us, 'Go drink at the spring ...' This spring is no
mere water. This spring is a symbol of Jesus himself. He is 'living water'. And Jesus will not let us
go home thirsty. He wants us to drink, to have
our fill. He wants to revive the 'drooping spirit'.
In 1966, a local French priest wrote a hymn in
honour of Bernadette: 'With you, Bernadette, we
walk towards the spring of living water.' With
Bernadette, thousands of pilgrims walk every
day towards the spring. It is a source of healing
for the body but, more importantly, it is a source
of healing for the heart. We are reminded of the
Samaritan woman. We come to fetch water as

she did. We come sometimes tired and weary just as she was at Jacob's well. Here is a poor hurt woman whose heart had been deceived five times. Five love affairs gone astray. She could not love any more, and was no longer loved. Isn't that a desperate situation, the ultimate distress of a woman reduced at this point of her life to the drudgery of fetching water from the well in the midday sun? Isn't this a striking image of humanity, a humanity that no longer knows how to love and be loved? At the well Jesus waits for her. '*If you only knew the gift of God,*' he tells her. He gives her that gift. He opens her eyes to discover the love she is really yearning for. He revives her 'drooping spirit'. She realizes that Jesus is the answer to all her deepest desires. As we find ourselves at the feet of Mary, perhaps with tears in our eyes, perhaps crushed in spirit and in body, perhaps just lost from the rhyme and reason of life, Jesus waits. He waits to tell us, as he told the Samaritan, '*if you only knew the gift of God*'.

The spring was made known to Bernadette during the ninth apparition. That means right at the heart of the eighteen apparitions, right at the centre. It was during this apparition that Our

Lady also asked Bernadette to undertake a series of penitential gestures on behalf of sinners: 'Would you be so kind as to kiss the ground for sinners ... to crawl on your knees for sinners ... to eat the grass that is there for sinners ...' When the ninth apparition was taking place, it was Holy Week in Lourdes. So all the gestures that Bernadette makes are in reality a mime of the Passion. 'Kissing the ground' for sinners reminds us of Jesus embracing humanity in a kiss of life on the Cross. 'Crawling on the ground' of the times Jesus falls to the ground under the weight of the Cross. 'Eating the grass' recalls the eating of bitter herbs – the Passover meal of the sacrificial lamb. So all that surrounds the discovery of the spring, all that surrounds the symbolism of water, is related to Holy Week; it is related to the passion, death and resurrection of Jesus. The water flowing from the side of Christ on the Cross is his life poured out for us.

In life we have a passion for many things; for riches, for pleasure, for position, for power. We have a love of passion. In Jesus, it is utterly different. Not a love of passion but a passion of love. On one of my confessionals in Lourdes I used to have a poster. It was the image of a very simple cross. Underneath were written the words: 'It wasn't the nails that held Jesus to the Cross but his love for you and me.' It is this love for us that leads Jesus to the extreme, to lay down his life for us. It is the most radical attempt of all by God to convince us we are loved by him. But we take some convincing! *If you only knew the gift of God.*' The spring at Lourdes, and the context of its discovery, wants to remind us all again.

The Samaritan woman was far from thinking that someone was waiting for her. It seemed like just another routine day in her life. But something happens. There at the crossroads of her life comes an unexpected and unique experience. Jesus waits for her: *'Give me to drink,'* he asks. At Jacob's well it is the beginning of a new alliance. A Jew could never speak with a Samaritan. They were worlds apart in religion and culture. They were enemies. Jesus removes all the barriers that exist between him and the woman; the barriers of sex, race, nationality, morality and religious beliefs. The Samaritan woman is profoundly touched by him, by his goodness. There is no condemnation, no judgement. There is no hostility, only welcome, only care and concern. Jesus awakens her to the love she craves. He transforms her life.

Jacob's well is always present for us. It is here at Lourdes. It is here on all the roads we may travel. It is always *here* and now. It is here in our own personal moment of history that Jesus waits for us. He waits because he loves us. What is it like to wait for someone we love? Jesus gives us some idea in the story of the Prodigal Son. He speaks of a father who never ceases to wait, who always expects the son to return, whose only desire is to see his son back home again. God is not against us. He is never menacing, out to get us. His only desire is to give. We often speak of the desires of man. In the Bible everything begins with the desires of God for man. And his desire is to *'bless us in Christ with every spiritual blessing …'* (Eph 1:3)

God does not resent the gift of creation. He does not regret the fact that he gave us life. He made us because he loves us. I exist because God desires me. That desire continues. Even if we have never been faithful, even if we have done terrible things, even if we have wandered far 'from home,' the choice of God is always upon us. Moreover, he does not invite us merely into existence. He invites us to share in the very community of love that is himself, the community that is Trinity.

Even if your mother and father forget you, I never will.' (Isaiah 49:15) We are not forgotten. Jesus did not forget the Samaritan woman. He did not let her pass by unnoticed. On the contrary, he invited her back into existence. He was the one who asked her for friendship and dialogue. He was the one who removed the barriers that had paralyzed her heart. He freed her to live again, to love again.

He comes to do the same for us. When the prodigal returns to the father, there is no asking of explanations. There is no recrimination, no reproach. Instead there are only words of joy and celebration, for the *'one who was lost is found, the one who was dead has come alive again.'* Jesus does not want to reproach us, to threaten us, to punish us. He simply wants us to be 'found again, to come alive again.' (Lk 15:32)

At Jacob's well Jesus asked to drink. On the Cross he said, 'I am thirsty.' He is thirsty for our hearts, for our love. And he thirsts to give us his love, to remove the barriers that separate us from him and from each other. Lourdes, the spring at Massabielle, is a privileged place where God meets people. It is another Jacob's well. Jesus waits not to reproach but to welcome not to condemn but to save. Jesus waits. He waits to invite us back into existence, to tell us again *'if you only knew the gift of God.'*

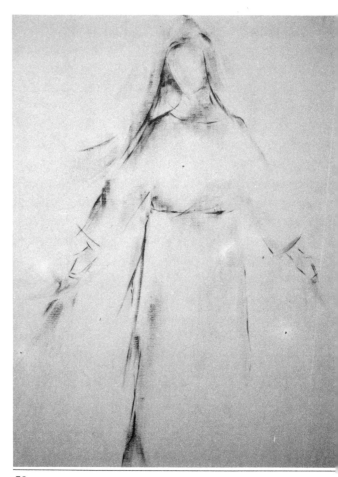

5. Let it Be

When I find myself in times of trouble,
Mother Mary comes to me,
speaking words of wisdom, let it be, let it be ...
And in my hour of darkness
she is standing there in front of me,
speaking words of wisdom, let it be, let it be ...

When the Beatles recorded this song in the early 60s they must have been reading the Bible. Whether the intention was religious or not, the words can be so easily applied to our own 'Mother Mary', the Blessed Virgin Mary. For Mary does have a great wisdom to give us in our times of trouble and darkness and in all the moments of our lives. That wisdom is made transparent in the words 'Let it be' – *'let it be done unto me according to your word.'* (Lk 1:38)

Sometimes we think because Mary is the Mother of Jesus, the Mother of God, Queen of heaven and earth, that she sailed through life without a problem. But this is not the Mary of the Gospels. We don't find her in her early life in Nazareth with a crown of twelve stars around her head, or with a beautiful white gown, blue sash and yellow roses on her feet. That's for later. In her earthly life, Mary knows problems and pain as we do. There are times when she doesn't understand, doesn't know how it will all work out. There is the real pain of seeing a son misunderstood and opposed; there is the agony of the crucifixion 'And a sword shall pierce your heart,' and a sword does pierce her heart. What is it that sustains Mary in these agonies of the heart? We are told by Elizabeth in the Gospel account of the Visitation: 'Blessed is she who believed that the promise made her by the Lord would be fulfilled.' (Lk 1:45) Elizabeth reveals to us the true greatness of Mary. She is the woman of faith, the one who truly believes in the word of God. She is 'Blessed among women' because she trusts in the word of God, in the promises of God. The word of God does not lie. What God has promised will be so. What God has said will come about, will indeed come about. Mary bases her whole life and hope in the word. Whatever the circumstances, whether she is led forward or backward, even into darkness and danger, even into the most agonizing of circumstances, Mary stands upon the word. It can never let her down. *'Let it be done unto me according to your word,'* – let everything unfold according to your word. Mary knows that God is the God of the real, that his plans unfold in the real events and situations we live. She faces that reality with God allowing the word to be her guide, her light, and her hope.

We don't always hear that word. Often communication between us and God is completely disrupted, completely broken down. One of the plagues of our time is noise. We watch a lot of television. It's the age of the image. That's how news and events come our way; not through the written word but through an instant image. The result is that we have no time for reflection, no time to stand back and assess, no time to listen. We are then cluttered up with so much that is unimportant and God is just drowned out, made absent. At Lourdes Mary speaks to Bernadette. She speaks a word that invites presence, a word that asks for dialogue. Her communication leads to communion. All of the Bible reveals the plans of God for humanity. It is the word of God that invites presence and dialogue from each us. It is the word that communicates, and desires to lead us to communion with God.

When I was a boy growing up in a predominantly Protestant Scotland, the Bible was considered as rather a Protestant affair. Somehow it was not for Catholics. Catholics were limited to more devotional practices like the recitation of prayers. Meditating upon the word of God was almost unthinkable. Not much has changed in our own times. Today we really need to rediscover a more Biblical spirituality. Bernadette herself said she 'only knew the rosary'. But what is the rosary? None other than a Gospel prayer, a prayer based on the word of God that centres on the main events in the life of Jesus. For too many of us, Sacred Scripture, the Bible is merely some written record of the past. We read it as a document that reveals the particular details of a particular people at a particular moment in history. We read it as critics, philosophers, historians or archaeologists. Faith takes us further. Faith demands we meditate on the word of God as believers. Consider the parable of the Sower in Luke's Gospel. We are shown that God's word is a divine seed. The divine seed is not a piece of writing! It is a living seed, a living word that must be sown in the fertile soil of our hearts. Are we fertile soil? Do we keep God's word as a living word, as a word that has meaning for us, as a word that is directed to us personally: to distinguish between the book we call and God's living word that is addresse personally in the actuality of our lives. Th ...ole is a living word. It is God speaking to us here and now. He speaks to us through Jesus above all, for everything has been brought together in him. We need to listen and not just read. There is no progress in our faith unless we listen to the word, unless we allow that word of God to give us a divine outlook on ourselves, on others, on the universe and above all on God. Look at the Blessed Virgin Mary. *'She pondered and treasured all these things in her heart.'* She gives everything time and space to unfold. Her pondering is not a stumbling in the dark but a quiet confident search for light and for meaning. Mary is the servant of the Word, of the Word that became flesh and dwells with people, of the Word that is the Light that has come into the world.

'Let it be done unto me according to your word.' We would like to have the faith of Mary. Instead we are more often like the two pilgrims who find themselves on the road to Emmaus. Like them we are 'slow to believe'. They cannot 'let it be'. They cannot 'let it be' because they stop at the

oss. They cannot see the Cross as being anything other than an end to their hopes and their dreams. They cannot 'let it be' any other way, for they have forgotten the promise of God. It takes a 'stranger' to remind them, to reawaken their hearts to what the whole of Scripture had proclaimed: *'Didn't you know that the Messiah had to suffer all these things and then enter into glory?'* Jesus reminds them that the Cross is not the end but the victory of love; it is a means of going further.

Shadowlands is a movie about the life of C.S. Lewis, a great Christian author. Professor at Oxford in the 1950s and 60s, he gave many conferences on suffering but somehow managed to remain immune from it. He had built up a sheltered world of familiar habit and routine. It is only when he falls in love that he begins to move out of his secure, insular life-style. And that love costs. It involves sorrow, especially when the woman he loves is diagnosed as having terminal cancer. He doesn't deny the sorrow. He enters into it. He embraces it. He suffers to love and love sustains and transforms the sorrow. The movie ends with C.S. Lewis uttering the poignant words: 'The boy chose safety, the man chooses suffering. The pain now, is part of the happiness, then. That's the deal!'

Yes, that's the deal. Sorrow and love are an inseparable part of the journey through life. Cross and glory are part of the one reality. Mostly we believe that we have to separate sorrow and pain because they are the opposite of the happiness we yearn for. Illness, death, the pains and aches of life have to be eliminated as they appear as an intrusion to happiness. In Jesus we find another way. In him the painful drama of our existence need not be denied. It can be embraced. It can be embraced not out of some masochistic desire to suffer, but out of the realization that from suffering new life can come forth.

Jesus chose the way of the Cross not to glorify suffering. He chose that way in order to reveal his Father's love. If Jesus had come among us clothed in magnificence and surrounded by legions of angels we would have been impressed. We would have recognized a mighty God. But that is about all. It would not really have touched our hearts. But a God who leaves all the security and beauty of heaven, who descends to live with us in our valley of tears and suffering, that is something else. Jesus comes not as the glorious Messiah of the earthly kingdom but as the suffering servant of love. It is only a suffering Jesus hanging on the cross who can reveal to what extent we are loved by the Father. The Father's love for us costs dearly, but he refuses us nothing. The Father's saying 'yes' to love means his own 'yes' to sorrow: 'Through the Cross Jesus paid the price, not so that we would not have to, but so that we would in fact know that there is a price for truth and love: everything.' (Richard Rohr in *Radical Grace*)

The story of Jesus is the story of every person. Saying 'yes' to love will involve saying 'yes' to sorrow. We need not run away from the terrible agonies that come our way. Jesus asks us to stand firmly on his word as Mary herself did. We can 'let it be,' not in fatalistic resignation to situations over which we have no control, but according to that word which promises that 'every tear will be wiped away'. If we stop at suffering we will be crushed. When we suffer to love Jesus is there and he will lead us from the cross to the victory of love. Jesus does not want us to be crushed by suffering. He invites us to trust in the midst of our agony, to abandon ourselves com-

pletely to a Father who will never ab/
am the Resurrection,' Jesus proclaims
present reality. Resurrection is not ·
the after life. It is for the here and now υ⌐ ·
personal lives. It is the power of the One who has
conquered all. It is the promise of never-ending
love. It is the promise of never being abandoned
to the darkness of our troubled hearts and circumstances. It is the promise that those who suffer to love will find the way to new life and hope.

*'Did not our hearts burn within us as he explained the
Scriptures to us?'* exclaimed the disciples of
Emmaus. Jesus did not abandon these poor men
to their poor faith. He explains, he opens their eyes
to see, he brings back hope and life. So it is for us.
He wants to open our eyes by means of his life
and his word. What happened in Lourdes happened well over a century ago. Bernadette is
long gone. But the memory of Bernadette and
the apparitions is still alive. It is not some mere
memory of the past. It is a memory that sustains
and gives life in the present. As we think of
Bernadette, of who she was, of how she lived her
life, we find much that gives meaning and nourishment to our lives today. So it is with the word
of God. This word is not a dead memory of the

st but a memory that sustains us here and now. Remember the advice the Blessed Virgin gave to Bernadette: '*Scrape away the soil and a spring will gush forth.*' We've read the Gospels, we've heard them. But we haven't scraped away the soil. We need to dig deeper. It is only the word of Jesus that will bring light in the darkness of our world. It is his word that will help us to create a little more hope in our world, a little more happiness, a little more love. '*When I find myself in times of trouble, Mother Mary comes to me, speaking words of wisdom, let it be, let it be, – let it be according to your word.*'

6. No Other Gods

Journalists, as the nature of their job demands, are always on the lookout for a 'good story.' That was so in 1858 as it is today. Bernadette was not just a good story. She was a sensational story. A child having visions of the Blessed Virgin Mary had captured the public imagination both in France and elsewhere in Europe. No journalist worth his salt could pass up such a golden opportunity. And so Bernadette was hounded by the media. One French journalist tried to persuade her to go with him to Paris. There, by relating the story of her meetings with the Blessed Virgin, Bernadette could exploit these events to her own advantage and in so doing make herself a lot of money. Bernadette refused. *'Money burns me,'* she said. Other journalists wrote articles about her frequently. Somebody asked her: How does it feel to have your name in print, to be a star, to be the centre of attention?' *'I don't know,'* said Bernadette, *'I can't read.'* Other people made other demands, like asking her to bless religious objects. *'I'm not a priest,'* was Bernadette's reply. These constant incursions into her life can be described as temptations, for that is what they are. They are temptations to power, wealth, success and position.

I find all this very reminiscent of the temptations made to Jesus by Satan in the desert. Satan, who says to Jesus: *'Change these stones into bread.'* In other words be relevant, turn everything to your own advantage. Satan who says to Jesus: *'Throw yourself down from the mountain.'* In other words be spectacular. Satan who says to Jesus: *'I will give you all these kingdoms.'* In other words be powerful.

Jesus, and Bernadette like him, reject all these temptations and for one reason only. God is the only source of their identity. They live the words of the first commandment: *'You will love the Lord your God with all your heart and all your strength. You will have no other gods before you.'*

'You will have no other gods before you.' Bernadette will allow nothing, not money or success or power or anything else to come before God. She was completely poor and could have used the

money. She was a nobody and could have used success to her advantage. But she refuses to do so. The Lord is first, her trust is in him alone. He will give her a greater treasure than money can buy. She sees that real security is not in wealth or position or power, but placing one's life within the most secure hands of all, those of God. There are no idols in Bernadette's life. She places nothing and no one before God. The Lord is first, the Lord is everything.

'*You will have no other gods before you.*' We may believe we are not prone to idolatry, but if we look closer at our lives, we most certainly are. Idolatry is not just about worshipping some statue carved by human hands, like the Jews and the golden calf. Idolatry has deeper and more subtle forms. It has deeper and more subtle forms but the object is always the same: the exaltation of ourselves. This is always the fundamental and dominant temptation: the aspiration of people to be 'like God'.

To understand temptation today we need to return to the Genesis accounts of creation and the expulsion of Adam and Eve from paradise. There we can rediscover what in fact constitutes the first temptation.

After the work of creating man and woman God rests. He rests not just because everything has been accomplished. He rests secure in the knowledge that he can leave all to man and woman. He rests above all because he trusts them. He places his confidence in them. There is a bond of love, a covenant between them. But instead of adoring they turn away from God. How does this breakdown of love occur? It is revealed to us in the symbolic story of the serpent, the woman and the dialogue between the two. Satan wants to break the bonds of love. This is what he always tries to do. He breaks the bonds of love with God. He breaks the human bonds of love. He sows discontent. In this case he tries to infiltrate the intelligence of the woman, to seduce her, to get her to accept him as her intellectual master. Only in this way can he achieve his objective: to ensure there is no dependency of love on the Love of God. *'You will not eat of the fruit of the tree that is in the middle of the garden, nor shall you touch it, or you shall die.'* (Gen 3:3) This is the only condition of the covenant that God makes with the man and the woman. Satan appeals to the woman's intelligence to bring revolt: *'You will not die … you will be like God, knowing good and evil.'* (Gen 3:4-5) In other words, he tells her to wisen up', to 'be smart', that God is holding out on them because he doesn't want them to have a knowledge that will enable them to decide life for themselves. He seduces Eve to equate herself with God, to be identical with God and so she does not need to obey, doesn't need to kneel before any other greater authority. So the first moment of separation from God occurs under the influence of the devil who deceives us into thinking we can save ourselves by our own intelligence. Man saves himself by himself. With the knowledge of good and evil he can work it all out for himself, he can judge what is right and wrong, what is good and evil. Here we have the exaltation of the intelligence, and the bonds of love are broken as a result. If the sin of Satan is pride, if Satan is someone who no longer loves, then he has no other ambition except to make us his disciples and to share in his prideful vision. Eve's sin is one of pride and not of a sexual nature. Satan wasn't kicked out of heaven for sins of the flesh but for the sin of pride. It is a sin not of the body but of the spirit, it is a sin of exalting himself to the detriment of love. And Eve shares the sin. Instead of realizing the greatness of the covenant of love God makes with them, the man and the woman prefer to listen to the evil one. They prefer their own experience and the exaltation of their own intelligence to the covenant of love that united them with God.

'You will have no other gods before you.' Idolatry is very much part of our lives today. What we need to do is recognize it. Notice the exaggerated exaltation of questioning in modern society. Just think of the number of television programmes that engage in in-depth analysis. Some people want to appear very intelligent by questioning everything. Today we question and question but we don't seem to conclude, to reach the truth; there is just interrogation and endless research. Yes, we have an intelligence. It is given by God and is there to be used. But it is there to be used as a humble servant of love and truth and not for inflating our already overinflated egos. It is to be used in the knowledge that it is not our property but a precious gift given to us by Another and will bear fruit only when guided by his Spirit *'who will teach us everything and lead us to the truth.'* (Jn 14:25) To the lawyer who continually questions Jesus as to the means of obtaining eternal life, Jesus replies with the story of the Good Samaritan (Lk 10:25-37). The means of finding life is not in the realm of the intellectual, but by moving out from oneself and loving.

Humanity wishes to save itself without God, and hence without love. Humanity claims to save humanity through science, through technology. Modern pseudo-philosophical cult movements such as New Age reveal the same temptation of humanity to exalt itself. However, 'New Age' only leads to old age since it is built on the perennial illusion that a person by himself or herself can save, heal, find peace, and find the answers in their own hearts to the deeper yearnings of the heart. No, we cannot build our own paradise. That is an illusion but one hard to shake off. We still believe that by hoarding up wealth and possessions we will find security and happiness. There is nothing wrong in improving the quality of life. We have a duty to do so. There is hence nothing wrong with wealth and possessions in themselves. The problem is how we see them and how we use them. The problem is that they often dictate how we live and dominate our lives rather than the opposite. We put our trust and our hopes in something that is here today and gone tomorrow, and fail to realize that our only real identity lies in God, that our true value lies in his love for us, in our response to that love, and not in what we may or may not have. Or we place all our hopes, expectations and dreams on another human being, as if a sinful limited creature like ourselves could ever satisfy all the longings of the human heart.

'He went into the Temple and he began driving out those who were buying and selling there ... You have turned this place into a robbers den ... My house is a house of prayer.' (Mt 21:12-14)

The temple was so important in the life of the Jews. Here was the place where God dwelt among them. It was the symbol of the whole spiritual dimension of their lives. The Temple represented the whole Jewish religion. At the time of Jesus it had become empty, without heart. It was no longer the expression of the presence of God. It had become all too human and certainly stagnant. The rabbis of the time had taken the place of God. Their claim to follow God was more outward than inward. Jesus appears on the scene and calls people back to the true sense of Temple the place of God's presence – and that nothing else can occupy this place. In the Father's house there can be no commerce: nothing and no one can occupy the place reserved to God alone.

Jesus went even further. He went far beyond what the Jews understood by Temple. In another

assage of the Gospels he speaks to the Samar-
an woman. There had always been a feud
etween the Jews and the Samaritans over who
wned the real Temple: was it on a mountain in
amaria or was it in Jerusalem. The answer Jesus
ives points to something deeper. *'The time is
ming,'* he said, *'when neither on this mountain or
 Jerusalem that you will worship the Father ...
 stead you will worship him in spirit and in truth.'*
 n 4:21-24) In other words, we will worship the
ather in our hearts. It is the heart that becomes
 e temple of God. Jesus tells us that we need to
uild our lives on his presence, that nothing and
 o one can occupy the first place except God. Not
 ealth, not possessions or position. Nor can any
uman being be first in our lives. Not our hus-
and, our wife, our children, our friends. Only
 e Lord can be Lord. Jesus says: *'Whoever prefers
 ther or mother, husband and wife to me is not wor-
 y of me.'* (Lk 14:26) When he says these things
 e is not putting before us the choice of two
 ves. He is not saying to us, 'father or me, wife
 r me, etc.' He is telling us that there is only one
 ve and that within this one love are found all
 ur other loves. He is telling us that we can only
ver say 'I love you' to someone if it is rooted
 ithin the one who is source of all love.

Without someone greater than we are to giv
meaning to our little lives, we die in our own illu:
ions. Without a greater love to refer to, we becom
lost in our own private limited world. Withou
another who 'ranks ahead' of us, we quickly exa
our own intelligence and follow the blind judge
ments of our own ego. And when that happen,
the bonds of love between ourselves and God ar
broken. And when the bonds of love are broke
we are in the greatest danger.

It is fifty years since Auschwitz. Televisio
brought the commemoration of events there int
our homes. I saw a woman being interviewed. '
is fifty years since I was here,' she said, 'but I fee
that I have never left. The experience has alway
been with me.' She spoke of the atrocities. At th
end of her account she said, 'and to think tha
man is capable of all this!' I can still see the face c
this woman, the immense pain in her eyes, th
voice repeating over and over: 'And man i
capable of all this!' What man did she mean? Th
Germans? No doubt. But the meaning is wide
She didn't use the word Germans. She used th
more general term 'man'. She meant all of us. W
are all capable of horrors like this. The German
were seemingly ordinary people just like u:

hey were fathers and brothers, they had children and sisters. We can't imagine that we could do to people what they did to the Jews. But we are capable of it. The Nazi extermination of the Jews is the most flagrant example of humanity's exaltation of itself. It happens when the only God we believe in is our own ego. It happens when we make ourselves the measure of all. It happens when we have no noble vision of love to sustain us and guide us. Then we wander in the desert of darkness, illusion and self delusion. In the desert we end up not only 'with the wild beasts' (Mk 1:12) but as the wild beasts.

It's in the desert that Jesus is tempted. He allows himself to be tempted. He allows himself to go hungry. By so doing he reveals his desire to identify completely with the human condition. He knows the hungers we have. He knows that in the 'desert', the 'desert' of the cold impersonal world in which we live, the desert of pain and difficulty, the desert of darkness and confusion, Satan comes to seduce us, holding out to us in attractive ways what appears to be the means to secure present and future happiness. Jesus allows himself to be tempted and go hungry to enable us to respond to those temptations as he

himself did. His only concern is that we are no
seduced to take life in our own hands but t
remain firmly within the hands that created u
and hold us eternally in an embrace of love
Jesus points us away from humanity's vision o
humanity to behold God's vision of humanity. I
is a vision that indeed proclaims that humanit
can become 'like God', but not through prid
and self exaltation. We become like God only i
the measure that we become as God in Jesu
reveals himself to be: that is as the poor, humble
suffering servant of love. Asked if she was
saint, Bernadette replied: *'No, I'm not a saint. I'*
just a broom in the hands of the Virgin Mary. Whe
you've finished with the broom you put it behind th
door. That's its place.' No self-exaltation. Sh
knows her place. She knows the place of God i
her life. She has 'no other Gods.'

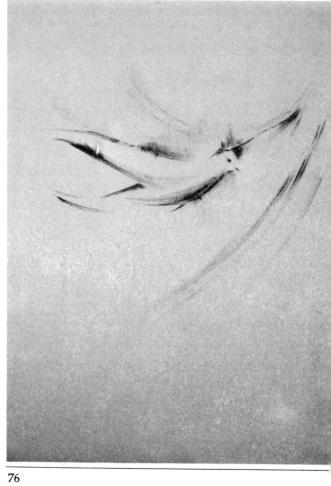

7. When the Spirit moves

A cold sombre dawn heralded the arrival of February 11 1858. Dark clouds hung heavy in the sky over Massabielle. The inclemency of the day was not confined to the weather. Dark clouds hung heavy upon a child's heart. Sickness, suffering, poverty, destitution; these were the more hostile elements that clouded Bernadette's life. It was a time of impasse, dead ends, heavy burdens. We all know the feeling. We all have days like this. Sometimes the days stretch into months, sometimes even years. We reach the crossroads of impossibility, situations that lie heavy upon us with no apparent hope of solution. For Bernadette life had come to this. Humanly speaking this was the end of the road. By herself she could not find the way forward. By herself she could not create new life. That can only come from another greater than we are, one who never stops thinking about us.

And come it did. It all began with *'a sound like a*

ind,' Bernadette said. Words reminiscen
:cost. Dead situations need the breath o
:it to bring new life. In the chaos of her lif
the Spirit moves. Light begins to dispel the dark
ness. Heaven embraces earth and the whole o
Bernadette's life is changed, transformed, trans
figured. Poverty and sickness remain. The appari
tions do not change this. What changes is how i
is all lived. In the hands of the Spirit, the way o
poverty and suffering become the fertile ground
of an ever-deepening journey in the ways o
Jesus and holiness of heart. In the hands of the
Spirit, the impossible dreams of a child to
become a nun blossom into definite reality. He
way is made clear. Bernadette can and will
embrace the religious life. Massabielle, the 'old
rock,' the 'rubbish dump,' the 'pig-sty,' will rise to
heights never imagined. Upon this '*rock*' the
chapel is built. Lourdes will flourish and become
what it is today, a place of hope and prayer for
the many who come from all over the world to
adore the God who is 'the rock secure on which
to build.'

We live in an age of great anguish. Many tradi-
tional values have broken down both in the
Church and in society. Authority and institut-
ions that yesterday gave guidance and direction

are today rife with division or constantly oned. The plurality of ideas and opinic abound in society and in the Church can leave us confused. We are unsure of the road before us. We are often in a dilemma as to whose authority we can accept. While renewal is vital, relativity can easily be fatal. When there is no reference other than our own limited selves, life can easily degenerate into chaos. In the age of the in-depth analysis, we criticize and question, bisect and trisect. We have much to discuss but few solutions to offer. We are often left with nothing to hold on to. We throw out certain principles and structures but have nothing to offer by way of replacement. All of which tends to make us feel bewildered and very alone as we face the complexities of modern life. Yet this very bewilderment and isolation, instead of leading to despair and discouragement, can become for us a springboard to a new and more authentic living of the Christian message. For it is only when we are poor that the Spirit comes to us. If we truly accept our poverty, our littleness, our sense of helplessness, then we can begin to open our hearts to the presence of the Spirit. More readily we can depend on the Spirit to heal us and to guide us.

Before the empty tomb Mary Magdalene weeps.
She weeps not because Jesus is dead. She weeps
because she cannot find him, she doesn't know
where they have put him. Today we can so easily
weep with her when we look around our Church
and wonder where they have put the Spirit of
Jesus. Some time ago, when discussing the question of how bishops were elected, a leading
prelate in the Church said to me: 'Well you know
how it is today. It's all about having the right
connections!' The 'right connections' he meant
were people of power and influence. Poor me.
had always thought that the only 'right connect-
ion' was the presence of the Holy Spirit filling
the heart of a man to live the message of the
gospels and making it clear to all concerned that
the choice of God was upon him. The Holy
Spirit, the Father of the poor, cannot be present
where poverty isn't present. As soon as we love
power and position more than the truth, then the
Holy Spirit can do nothing with us. He will do
everything for us only if we cry out to him in our
need. Only when we cry out our fundamental
hunger to love and to be loved will he lead us
into true love, into a real and deep experience of
the Father. 'Go tell the priests to build the Church'
Mary said to Bernadette. The Church Our Lady

desires is certainly not the cold power-orientated impersonal institution, but a humble community of believers alive with the spirit of Jesus' love. In the beginning of creation it is the Spirit who moves over the 'formless void, the chaos' and brings order and life. Only the Spirit can bring order from the chaos within our own hearts and around us, within our society and within the Church.

When we think of Pentecost, we always think of the charismatic Pentecost described in the Acts of the Apostles. That's not surprising since it attracted a lot of attention. But isn't there another Pentecost that comes before this, that happens with Jesus, only this time in silence and in the desert? *'I saw the Spirit descend on him like a dove and remain on him.'* (Jn 1:32) The Spirit remains upon him. We have a gift that is lasting. No passover of God here. No God passing by, no passing of the Spirit. The Spirit remains. *'I will not leave you orphans ... the Holy Spirit, whom the Father will send in my name, will teach you every-thing and remind you of all that I have said to you.'* (Jn 14:11-18) The Holy Spirit is not a gift reserved to those claiming adherence to the charismatic renewal. It is a gift given in baptism and confirmation to all followers of Jesus. It is a gift given to enable us to live our Christian life. We sometimes see that life as impossible to live, or only for the 'saints'. How can we really love our enemies? How can we bless those who persecute us? How can we love one another as Jesus loved us? How can we possibly be 'compassionate as the heavenly Father is compassionate'?

Jesus does not invite us to do something and then not provide the power, the strength to do so. If he invites us to live completely and truly the message of the Gospels, then he will make us capable of doing so. If he invites us to be compassionate as the Father is compassionate, then he will empower us to live this reality, to live and love with the very tenderness of the Father's heart. It is the same for all that Jesus asks of us. He will empower us. We will be *clothed with power from above* (Lk 24:49) that is the gift of the Spirit promised by the Father. The Holy Spirit mobilizes all our strength, all our energy, and all our capacities toward the goal of increasing in love, towards the goal of contemplating God and towards the good of our neighbours.

Even in our worst moments, those times of utter desolation and impossibility, in those moments when prayer seems an empty gesture, it is the *Spirit who helps us in our weakness ... who intercedes for us with sighs too deep for words.'* (Rom 8:26) He is given to empower us to live our questions and complexities in the light of faith, to lead us through the hostile deserts of our troubled existence, to see that we are not at the mercy of events but always within the divine mercy. *'How will this come about?'* a troubled Mary asks the angel at the annunciation. *'The Holy Spirit will come upon you,'* is the answer. We may not know how things will work out in our lives. We may not know the final outcome of our problems or where it's all leading to. But the promise remains: *'I will not leave you orphans ...'* If we cry out in our need, if in our poverty and helplessness we abandon ourselves to the Spirit, he will *'come upon us'* to enlighten us and direct us, to make clear the path before us.

Bernadette was a true child of God. In the poverty and cry of her heart, the Spirit moved to lead her forward on the journey to greater intimacy with the Father. *'When we cry, "Abba! Father!" it is that very Spirit bearing witness with our spirit that we are children of God.'* (Rom 8:15-16) Today, as we begin to discover our radical need, our immense poverty; today in the impossibilities of our own lives, let us feel the movement of the Spirit in us that makes us cry out:

Our Father, may I today experience the heaven of love where you dwell;

may your name be sanctified and glorified in all my being and especially in this trial I am suffering;

May your kingdom come! May Jesus who revealed your kingdom become incarnate in all my difficulties.

May your will be done in all my pain on earth as it is in heaven!

Give me today my daily bread, the daily bread of your compassion, the daily bread that is a solution to my problems.

Forgive me all my sins, especially those that have led me to this situation, and forgive all those who by their sinful actions have also made me dwell in darkness;

And lead us not into temptation the temptation to discouragement, to despair, to walking away from your heart;

But deliver us from the evil one, from his lies, from his deceit. (see Lk 11)

Abba! Father! Send us the Spirit of love, the Father of the poor, the giver of all consolation.

8. Bad Catholics

There are many people who think that the opposite of being Catholic is Protestant. But the opposite of Catholic is not Protestant. Nor is it Anglican, Methodist, Hindu, Moslem or even atheist. Why is that so? It is so because the word *Catholic* means universal, all embracing, something wide that includes. So the opposite of Catholic is not Protestant. The opposite of Catholic is being intolerant, narrow-minded, bigoted and judgemental.

In the 1870s the Prussian armies were about to invade France. 'Aren't you afraid of the Prussians?' someone asked Bernadette. *'No, I'm not afraid of the Prussians,'* she replied, *'I'm only afraid of bad Catholics.'* Who are these bad Catholics that Bernadette refers to? She doesn't just mean sinners, for she describes herself as a sinner: 'Pray for me, a poor sinner,' she said. She places herself firmly in the ranks of sinners. So what does she mean by bad Catholics?

Bad Catholics are those who actually consider themselves to be good Catholics. These are the people who outwardly are religious but who have no truly religious heart. They are the people who follow all the religious practices, who know all the correct dogmas and doctrines but whose hearts are far from the ways of God. In our more humble moments, we can recognize ourselves within this group of people that Bernadette denounced. There is a lot of the bad Catholic in each of us. We can easily go to Church every day, frequent all the sacraments, and have no love and compassion. Outwardly we give all the appearances of being Christian. Inwardly we condemn all those around us. Privately we think we are good. Publicly we make sure that everyone knows the local gossip: that the next door neighbours are living in sin, that the guys down the street have aids, and that the local priest is having some scandalous love affair.

I often meet the bad Catholics in confession. 'I live a good life ... I go to Mass every day ... I've really nothing to tell you ...' That's how it begins. I usually answer by telling them that I don't have the faculty for canonization, only for confession! Or they are the ones who never confess their own sin but everyone else's. They quickly excuse themselves or direct attention from themselves by blaming every other agency for their own ills. It is always the fault of someone or something else – the Church, society, the world in general. I always direct them to the story of the Pharisee and the Publican for it has much to tell us. Let us consider again this famous Gospel story:

Two men went up to the temple to pray, one a Pharisee, the other a Publican. The Pharisee was praying thus: 'God, I thank you that I am not like other men ... I fast ... I give of my income ...' The Publican would not even look up to heaven, but was beating his breast and saying: 'God be merciful to me, a sinner!' 'I tell you this man went home justified rather than the other, for all who exalt themselves will be humbled, and all who humble themselves will be exalted.' (Lk 18: 9-14)

The two men start off well. Both begin with God. They put themselves in the presence of another; they appeal, call to the presence. The presence of God is invoked intensely. That's what we desire when we pray; we want the presence of God to fill our place of prayer, our thoughts, our hearts. We want God to fill all the minutes and moments of our rendezvous. But why does the prayer of the Pharisee fail and that of the Publican succeed? 'The publican went home justified.'

The Pharisee had followed the right procedures. He had invoked God but he follows up with an enormous 'I'. Here we have such an inflated ego, the great 'I am'; I am this, I am that, I am not like this, I am not like that, 'I am not like other men.' *I* is the first and God is a long way second.

The Publican instead touches the heart of God with his humble entreaty: 'Be merciful.' God revealed by Jesus is a God of mercy. He looks at us with mercy. He looks at us in the pity of love. An understanding touches his heart when he sees our hearts are moved: *'a humble, contrite heart he will not spurn.'* (Psalm 50) The mercy of God is not general, vague. It waits on our cry and has pity. In the presence of God the Publican remains small, humble. In this he can introduce his 'I' (me). But it has last place in his prayer: 'God, be merciful to me, a sinner.' Christian prayer is a rendezvous of love. It's about the *You* of God and *me*. But how we need to be careful that the *you* is first and immense, and our *me* definitely last.

So the parable opens up on a man who does a lot, who is sure of himself, and who believes himself right in God's eyes. The parable closes on a man sure about God and is made right in God's eyes only because he knows how to say 'be merciful'. A very good fictional story further enlightens and clarifies:

There is a prophet who is on his way to the mountain to speak with God. Along the road he meets a hobo leaning against a wall. He approaches the hobo and tells him how much he is loved by God. At this the hobo jumps up and down, dancing with joy. Sometime later the prophet meets a Pharisee along the same road. He tells him also how much he is loved by God, and the Pharisee, like the hobo before him, also jumps up and down, dancing with joy. Some months later, the prophet goes back up the mountain to converse with his God. He inquires about the hobo and the Pharisee. What had become of them? And God answers: 'Well the hobo is with me here in heaven. Sadly the Pharisee is in hell.' 'But how can that be?' asks the prophet, 'I gave them both the same message and both jumped for joy.' 'Ah yes,' said God, 'but the hobo danced with joy because he knew I had remembered him. The

Pharisee, on the other hand, danced for joy because he felt he had done everything well!' For the first time in his life the prophet wondered which path he was on: that of heaven or that of hell.

It is a striking story. Which path are we on ourselves? We need to uproot from our hearts the pharisaic belief that we attain salvation by our own efforts. We need to cultivate a more publican heart that recognizes our need to cry out for mercy. We do not recognize our sin because we do not recognize love. When we come to confess our sins our first task is not an examination of conscience. It is rather an examination of confidence; that we begin by looking at the immense love God holds out to us, and in the light of that love we can examine our own poor lives. It is only when we grasp God's love for us that we can see ourselves as the sinners that we are.

The bad Catholics that Bernadette denounced are those who believe they are always in order before God. Feeling no need of mercy themselves, they can no longer be merciful to others. They are those who proclaim with their lips that Jesus is Lord but in their hearts act as if they are Lord themselves. We are all often like this and especially when we place ourselves upon the throne in place of God and condemn and judge others.

There are times when we have the right to be angry. We have the right to point out evil and injustice. We have the right to take a stand against evil. But we have no right to allow our anger to lead to condemnation and intolerance. We need to separate the sin from the sinner. When we see ourselves as the sinners that we are, then instead of killing each other off, we can have greater compassion for one another. When we see that, in the eyes of God, none of our lives are in order but that he loves us just the same, then we can more easily welcome each other into our hearts. Bernadette placed herself in the ranks of the sinners. She gave her whole life for sinners: *'O Jesus and Mary, may my consolation in this world be to love you and suffer for sinners.'* She doesn't react with disgust at the ugliness around her but with compassion. Her concern is not to condemn but to save. There is a passage in the Book of Revelation where it says that the evil one accuses us night and day before the throne of God. He accuses and condemns. We play his part when we do the same. Jesus came into the world not to condemn but to save. He came with a catholic heart – a heart that is all-embracing, a heart that embraces the whole of sinful humankind. He wants us to live and to love with his heart – a heart that knows it has been remembered in mercy and is ready to render that mercy to others.

Bad Catholics or good? It is for each one of us to answer.

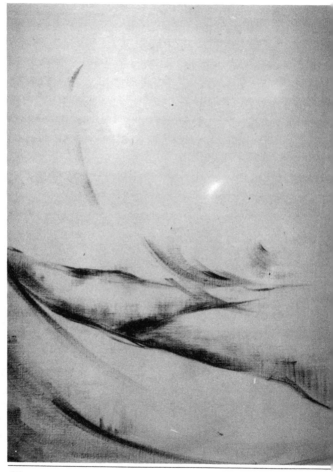

9. A Voice in the Wilderness

Bernadette and Lourdes. Bernadette and Bartrès. And in Bartrès the parish Church of St John the Baptist. It was a place where Bernadette liked to pray. It may seem strange that there could be any relationship between Bernadette and John the Baptist. They are separated by centuries, by geography, by race and by culture. Here are two very different people from two very different worlds. Yet they do have much in common. For both of them are prophets, messengers of God. A prophet is someone who has seen and heard something of heaven and is compelled to speak of it. Both Bernadette and John the Baptist fill the role very well.

John is the *voice of one crying in the wilderness, make straight the way of the Lord.* (Jn 1:23) Here is the prophet who announces the One who is to come. Here is the prophet who reveals the Messiah who is here. The mission of John is to reveal the presence of the Lamb to the world, a

presence the world no longer sees. *'Behold th*
Lamb of God who takes away the sin of the world.' (Jn
1:29) The God of all tenderness and mercy ha
come to deliver his people from oppression – no
the oppression of the Roman Empire or the cor
rupt religious authorities of the time. His deliv
erance is of a greater magnitude that spans th
whole of history and embraces humankin
throughout the ages. His deliverance is from th
oppression that lies at the heart of every oppres
sion, that of sin and evil. The God of mercy ha
heard *'the cry of the child in the desert'* (Gen 21:16
and has come to them in their poverty and mis
ery to bring Good News to the poor. Jesus is her
to announce a new alliance between God and hi
people, an alliance made possible and sealed i
his own blood, an everlasting alliance of lov
with the Father. The prophet cries out in th
wilderness to open our hearts to this reality, t
call us to repent, to change, to welcome Jesus a
Saviour, as the Way, the Truth and the Life.

'A prophet is never accepted in his own country
Jesus said. And it certainly applies to the Baptis
He is opposed by many. The wilderness Joh
finds himself in is not merely that of the physic
desert. Wilderness is a symbol of the inhospitabl

nd unwelcoming, the hostile and
ohn faces the dark and hostile force
cal and religious alliances of hi
Sanhedrin have no need of a Savio
convinced they can save themselves. They are in
smug self-satisfaction. They want no one who
ranks ahead' of them (Jn 1:30). It is only the poor
who can receive the Good News Jesus came to
announce. The religious and political leaders are
not poor. Spiritual and intellectual riches blind
their hearts. Pride and power are the only trea-
sures they want, and that prevent them from seeing their need of a saviour. These are the obstacles that make it impossible for them to welcome
the coming of Jesus into their hearts. John cries
out in the wilderness of opposition and danger.
He is the voice of the Holy Spirit. He is the voice
of the poor.

Bernadette, the child, the uneducated, the des-
pised, the poorest of the poor. Here is the chosen
instrument of God. Here is another voice that
cries out in the wilderness of our times. She sees
something of the 'invisible' world of heaven.
Like John the Baptist she beholds the reality of
God's tender love for humankind. She announces
the appearance of the Blessed Virgin Mary

g us. She reveals Mary's appeal for sinners convert, to return to the tender ways of God's love. In fulfilling her mission, she is opposed in the wilderness of her times as John the Baptist was in his. The political and ecclesiastical authorities give her a hard time. *'My job is just to give you the message,'* she says. *'It is up to you whether you believe it or not.'* The job of the prophet is always to deliver the message. Bernadette certainly did that. But do we believe, or what do we believe? Perhaps we need to hear again the voice of the child who cries out in the wilderness of our own day. Let us allow Bernadette herself to speak again to each of us in the depths of our own hearts :

'Our Lady chose me because I was the poorest and the most ignorant. The poor are the friends of God.'

One day, some years ago, I was walking through the streets of Lourdes in the company of a high-ranking churchman. Suddenly he stopped and said: 'Look at this place. It's just a spirituality for peasants.' I answered that if I could only be a peasant like Bernadette I would be well pleased. *'Thank you, Father, Lord of heaven and earth, because you have hidden these things from the wise and intelligent and have revealed them to children.'* (Lk 10:21)

In choosing Bernadette, God makes it clear that he prefers to place 'his glory' in the hands of those whom the world excludes and ignores. It is to them especially that he entrusts his name and the mystery of his love. It is from the poor, the lowly, the humiliated, those without a voice, that the face of God reveals itself to the world. God is not drawn to us by our greatness. He is drawn to us by our poverty, our littleness, our humility. When Mary proclaims the *Magnificat* she does not glorify the Lord because he looks on her as a wonderful person (although we know she is). No, instead Mary glorifies the Lord because '*he looks on her in her lowliness.*' It's in lowliness that we are honoured and loved by God. Only the poor of heart can truly welcome Jesus into their lives. Only the poor realize that everything is gift. Only the poor can recognize that Another 'ranks ahead' of them. When we are filled with spiritual and intellectual pride, with ourselves, with our power, position, and possessions, then there is no room for anyone else in our hearts. Jesus identifies himself with the poor. He identifies himself completely with what the world considers to be not only the most useless but even a curse – poverty, sickness, suffering: '*I was hungry and you gave me to eat … sick and you took care of me ... naked and you clothed me ...'* (cf Mt 25) Jesus himself is the poor one. He comes to us not with the trappings of the glory of the world but showing us his wounds and begging for our love. Just as he made his home in the poor humble cave of Bethlehem, so he prefers to make his home in the poor humble heart that has nothing of self to block the way. *'Blessed are the poor in heart for to them belongs the kingdom of heaven.'* (Mt 5:3)

'I love what is little.'
'Unless you become like little children, you will never enter the kingdom of heaven.' (Mt 18:3) Jesus himself is the first to live the reality of these words. He is the almighty God who makes himself little. Consider the infancy narrative of Luke's Gospel. Look at what the angel says to the shepherds: *'This will be a sign for you; you will find a child wrapped in bands of cloth and lying in a manger.'* (Lk 2:12) Can this possibly be the sign of God? A child in a manger? There is absolutely nothing spectacular or glorious. Who can possibly go beyond the appearance of a poor child in a manger and recognize that this is Jesus, Son of God? Yet this is the sign of God! The sign of God is here, revealed in poverty, littleness and humility. *'I love what is little,'* Bernadette said. These words

are an appeal for us to discover, as Bernadette herself did, the depths and hidden riches of those who have no appearance, who are little considered in the eyes of the world. In discovering the spring at Lourdes, Bernadette has to scrape away the soil. We too need to dig below the surface, to look beyond the mere appearance to find the 'signs of God' that dwell in our midst. In his book, *Followers of Jesus*, the famous author of the L'Arche communities for the handicapped, Jean Vanier, relates an experience he had in India. He was walking down a road. On one side of the road was the most miserable filth and squalor where the poor had set up home. On the other side of the road was a modern seminary with every comfort. 'On which side of the road would Jesus live?' asks Jean Vanier. What a question! On which side of the road do we live? Do we like Bernadette truly 'love what is little'?

'She looked at me as one person looks at another.'
'She said to me: "would you be so kind as to..."'
'I looked at her all I could.'

We experience daily the feeling of other peoples' indifference, distrust, neglect or meanness. Bernadette discovers in Our Lady an attitude of infinite respect. Mary reveals to Bernadette the infinite respect and tenderness God has for his little ones. A look of love from Mary, a word of tender respect, makes Bernadette feel welcomed and wanted. She is noticed and cared for. She is held in the embrace of a personal and deeply loving relationship. *'I remember a summer that I could have lived on the look of love. You know it if you've experienced it. Somehow things that could be a pain or a burden are a joy because you know you're loved. You know your life has a meaning, you know someone loves you ... someone out there thinks you're lovable. Just thinking about that and knowing it makes the rest easy to take. The look of love is what each person lives for.'* (Richard Rohr in *Radical Grace*) How do we look at each other? As strangers, as enemies, as objects, as rivals, or as brothers on the same journey?

'Hide me, Jesus, in your Sacred Heart.'
'I came here to hide.'

'Hide' is one of the key words in Bernadette's spirituality. She uses it over and over again. In one sense it is not an escape from the world because she realizes that only by remaining within the heart of Jesus can we truly love and learn to love the world around us. But in another sense it is an escape from the world, an escape from a very particular world. It is a flight from that world that sought to confer upon her 'star status'. And to that she is definitely opposed. '*He must increase and I must decrease*,' she says quoting the words of John the Baptist. The mission of John is not to proclaim himself but to reveal a presence the world no longer sees. For Bernadette the mission is the same, even if it unfolds in a very different way. It is in her hidden life, her poverty, her humility, that she can reveal as no other can the greatness of God's love. I look at a child who, in a life hidden with Jesus behind the walls of a convent, touches the lives of millions and leads them to God. This is the voice of one who cries in the wilderness, questioning all our values and pointing us in other directions.

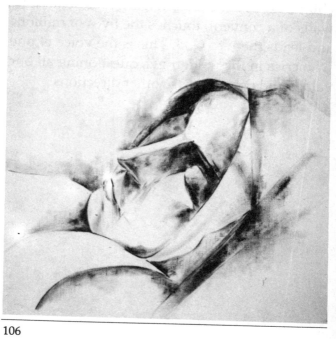

0. 'Happier than a Queen'

*appy are the poor in spirit, for to them belongs the
ngdom of heaven.*
*appy are those who hunger and thirst for what is
ght, for they will be filled.*
*appy are those who weep, for they shall be comfort-
l.* (see Mt 5)

an we continue to say 'happy are the poor' when
estitution and unemployment touch the lives
f millions of people?

an we continue to say 'happy those who hunger'
hen entire populations suffer from starvation,
d justice is continually denied in countries
ith oppressive regimes?

an we proclaim the happiness of 'those who
eep' when war and violence lead to blood baths
so many countries?

Jesus preaching passivity and fatalistic resig-
ation and pointing to heaven as a panacea for

those who find the earth insufferable? No, Jesus does not preach passivity or fatalistic resignation. Nor does he want us to focus our attention on the after-life and ignore the here and now. God may allow certain situations to be. But that does not mean he wants them to be. Much of the suffering we see in the world around us is often the result of humanity's own folly. Much of the injustice, oppression and violence, the denial of basic human rights is down to our own negligence and crime. That is our sin. We cannot blame God for the cruelty we are quite capable of inflicting upon ourselves. He certainly does not want us to act in this way. What he wants is that we work together in fraternal love in order to create a better world in which mercy, justice and equity prevail and where the dignity and freedom of every human being is promoted and respected. That's what God wants. He gave us the gift of freedom and he respects that freedom even when we abuse it. We can either create heaven or we can create hell.

No, Jesus does not preach passivity or fatal resignation. *'Love one another as I have loved you,'* is not a call to passivity. It is a command to give oneself actively and totally for the well-being of every one else even to the point of sacrificing one's own life. The Beatitudes, this hymn of happiness, was spoken by Jesus on a mountain in Galilee. It was not merely fine words from a good preacher. He did not remain on the hill after the sermon. He went down from the mountain. He descended to live these words with us in the valley of our own tears and suffering. The Beatitudes are a self-portrait. Jesus is the first to live them. It is his life that gives them meaning, his death their value, his resurrection their victory. They are an expression of his love, a love that is alive and personally engaged. They challenge us to reject the illusions of happiness offered by the world. They challenge us to realize that love is the only true power. They challenge us to trust in a goodness and a life beyond our own.

'Blessed are those who are well off. Happy are they who have money and comfort. Happy are those who are powerful, the people of influence. Happy are the young and the healthy.' These are the beatitudes of the society in which we live today. They are the beatitudes put before us every day in the media, in image and in word. In themselves they can never constitute true happiness. How can we be happy if even one person on the planet suffers? How can we be happy if

we have everything and others have nothing
Happiness lies more in the order of giving than
getting. It demands that we go beyond the limit
of our own self- gratification and smug self-satis
faction. Happiness is not in the power to domin
ate but in the humility to serve. The kingdoms o
this world are about hoarding. The kingdom o
heaven is about sharing. Happiness is not seeing
how rich we are. It is recognizing how poor w
are. That all is a gift. We are not the bosses, jus
the stewards. Happiness is not the denial of suf
fering. It is suffering to love, and loving to eas
the suffering, and transform it into new life. Thi
is what Jesus preached and there is nothing pas
sive here.

Jesus sees a new humanity being born not in th
powerful, the influential or the well off. He see
a new humanity being born amongst those wh
are not eaten up by abundance – in those wh
suffer, in those starved of justice, in those wh
struggle for peace, amongst those who ar
strong enough to be humble. Those who hav
their fill and rest content in their plenty cannc
hear the cry of the poor. Only those who them
selves are poor in heart can struggle to create
better world. Bernadette is one of those poor. Sh
is part of the new humanity Jesus came to creat

I am happier on my sick bed with my crucifix in my and than a queen upon her throne,' she said. She is not happy to be sick. She is not happy to suffer. She said so herself and very clearly. The reason for her happiness lies in what she holds in her hand: not the crucifix itself, but what the Cross symbolizes. Here is the embrace of love for all humankind, the victory of love over all suffering, darkness and death. It is the victory of humility over arrogance; the triumph of self-sacrifice over self-seeking; the reign of goodness over evil. Bernadette can remain 'happy' for she knows that in her sickness she is loved and held. And she knows her sickness can never be terminal. In Jesus love never dies.

'I do not promise you the happiness of this world but the other,' Our Lady said to Bernadette. This is not happiness for the next life, for the hereafter. It is not happiness promised to Bernadette as a reward in heaven for having suffered so much on earth. No, this is a happiness that comes from God alone and is given to her here and now. It is a share in the happiness won for us by Jesus. We share in that happiness when we, like him, struggle to allow love the victory in all times and in all circumstances.

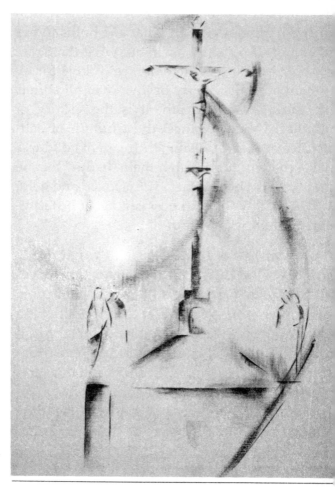

11. Sign Language

'Long ago God spoke to our ancestors in many and various ways through the prophets, but in these last days he has spoken to us through his Son ...' (Heb :1-2)

God speaks a word and the world comes into being. He speaks a word through the prophets and reveals himself to his people. Finally he speaks the last Word, the Word that is Jesus. He reveals all he is, and all we are called to live, in the person of his own Son. *'The Word was made flesh and dwelt among us.'* We believe in a God who speaks. His word is an invitation to existence, to dialogue, to communion. Sometimes we don't always hear that word. And since we don't hear it, we cannot enter into dialogue or communion. We are like the deaf and dumb, unable to hear, unable to speak, not in the physical sense but in the depths of our hearts. God knows our handicaps. He doesn't leave us in our deafness or our dumbness. In the 'many and various

aks, he gives us another lang-
hat only the deaf and the dumb
sign language!

f Lourdes comes to us in many
e important are poverty, mountain
(rock, ~   water and light. They are all outward signs of a deeper spiritual reality that God
wishes to work in our hearts. They are great
signs, powerful signs that can communicate to
us an ever deeper understanding of the message.
But for that to take place, they have to be understood within the context of the Bible and especially the Gospels. Let's take a closer look at these
signs:

POVERTY is the first sign. On February 11 1858 it is
poverty that forces Bernadette to leave home in
search of firewood. It is poverty that brings her
to the deserted place of Massabielle. And there at
Massabielle the Lady waits for her.

It was poverty, need, that led the Samaritan
woman to fetch water in the desert at Jacob's
well and there Jesus waited for her.

It was poverty that led the Israelites through the
desert as they searched for the promised land. It
is in that desert that God waits for them and with
them makes an alliance.

We have the spirituality of the desert. God who offers his presence and his friendship to those who wander poor and in need through the desert of the world in search of life.

MOUNTAIN is the second of the signs. At the foot of the Pyrenean mountains, in a cave in the rock known as Massabielle, a Lady, enveloped in light, smiles and welcomes Bernadette with open arms. We pilgrims come to stand before his cave where Mary appeared. Daily we kiss and touch the rock where she made herself known to Bernadette. Often we don't realize all that it means.

The mountain, the rock, the cave, is a powerful biblical sign. We are led to Sinai (Ex 19) and Horeb (1 Kings 19). The mountain is the place where God dwells. It is the place where he reveals himself. His Temple is built on the mountain and dominates the city. It will be on the mountain that the heavenly Jerusalem will descend from above (Ez 40:2; Rev 21:10-11). The ROCK is the symbol of the fidelity of God: *'God is my rock, my fortress.'* (Ps 17:3) The CAVE, the GROTTO, is the heart of the mountain where even in primitive times was the place of meeting with the cosmic forces. In the Bible, Moses and Elijah are admitted into intimacy with God as they find themselves in a cave. These great prophets are the principal witnesses of the God who makes himself known on the mountain.

In Lourdes, Mary now replaces the prophets. For she is the first witness of the Incarnation. She appears in a cave to remind us that the Word was made flesh and dwells among us. Jesus, born in a cave at Bethlehem, reveals himself to human kind.

WATER is the third sign. For many who come to Lourdes it is the only sign. Sadly it is perhaps the least understood. There are people who can go to the baths as many as six times in one day. We know cleanliness is next to Godliness, but that's pushing it a bit too far. I remember a little boy who went into the children's baths and started screaming, 'she's not my mamma!' It seems that nine different women had pretended to be this boy's mother so they could get into the baths before anyone else. I even heard the story of a farmer giving his pigs Lourdes water to drink so they wouldn't get sick. This is just nonsense. Not only is it not Christian. It is downright pagan. And this is what happens when we do not understand what the symbolism of this water means. When we don't understand, we run the risk of falling into superstition and magic.

All kinds of scientific studies have been made on this water. The results of these tests show the water to be just that: there are no special properties, no special healing agents. It's just pure simple water. The water itself is not miraculous. If the water was miraculous in itself, then anyone and everyone who touched this water would be healed. In that case there would be no need of faith, God or otherwise. It is not the water that heals – only God heals. He may use the water but it is only he who heals. It is true that many of the recognized cures of Lourdes have been associated with the water. But people have also been healed in other circumstances: during the processions, while receiving communion, while on the train or plane going home. Some have even been healed a few days after the pilgrimage while at home. In other words, there is no one element that heals. God alone heals. In all these elements the one common factor is God. Consider the Gospel story of the cripple who is lying near the pool of Siloe (Jn 5). He complains to Jesus that he has no one to put him in the water when it moves; for it is only when the water moves that healing takes place. When God moves the water then comes the healing. So it is with the water of Lourdes. It is only when God touches the water that healing comes about.

To really understand the meaning of this sign we have to see it in a biblical context and within the context of the wider message of Lourdes that goes beyond the physical to the spiritual. Lourdes speaks of the healing of the heart more than of the body. So too does the Bible.

We are reminded of the 'living water' promised to the Samaritan (Jn 4:10-14), to all those who are thirsty (Jn 7:37). The water that is a sign of the permanent reality of our baptism and of life in the Holy Spirit (Jn 7:38-39). The whole meaning of the water is about moving away from sin and finding new life in Jesus. 'What is it better I say to you: "get up and walk" or "your sins are forgiven you"?' (Mk 2:9) While Jesus is interested in the whole person, both body and spirit, the sign of the water is much more about the spirit than it is about the body.

LIGHT is the fourth sign. On Sunday February 28 at the end of the 12th apparition, Bernadette feels a need to leave something of herself at the

Grotto. She leaves the candle she had been holding in her hand. It has been the first of many in a long series as, day after day, year after year, pilgrims leave candles burning at the Grotto. They are little flames but with a very profound meaning. They are signs of faith and of Christian prayer. We are reminded of the Paschal candle, itself a sign of the Risen Christ. We are reminded of the tongues of flame at Pentecost (Acts 2:13), the burning bush of Moses (Ex 3). Above all we are reminded of Jesus, the *Light of the World.*' (Jn 8:12)

We are reminded also of the mission given to each one of us by Jesus: *'You are the light of the world.'* Each evening procession in Lourdes ends with the words: 'You are the light of the world, go carry the light to your brothers.' We are light? It can't be serious. We, with all our dark past and sinful present, we are light? Are we any better than others? No, we are not. We are just earthen vessels like everyone else. But there is a difference. We are earthen vessels who carry a treasure. The treasure is the word of whom we are servants. We cannot confuse the vessel with the treasure. We cannot equate that word to our own limited vision. We cannot water it down to accommodate the world. Nor can we keep it for ourselves as if it was our own property. We cannot hide the light under the 'bushel'. (Lk 8:16) Bernadette was a simple lay person chosen by Our Lady to go and give a message to the world. We are chosen also. We each have a role to play. When we pass from one country to another we find at the frontier the sign, 'Have you anything to declare?' Sometimes fear and compromise with the world prevents us from 'declaring.' Bernadette had her fears and her world also to contend with, but another power gives her the courage and the strength to give the message she is asked to give: *'There was something in me which helped me overcome the obstacles. I was pressed on all sides but never overcome.'* That's what she said. It is a strength promised to all of us by Jesus: *'Do not worry beforehand what you are to say ... but say whatever is given to you at that time, for it is not you who speak, but the Holy Spirit.'* (Mk 13:11) We do not need to stop at the frontiers of fear and pressure from the world. We have much to declare. We have much to declare for we are marked with another sign – the sign of the Cross. It is not the sign of defeat but of victory. It is the sign with which Our Lady and Bernadette first entered into contact. As Bernadette tried to make this sign she was afraid; we are always afraid before the unknown. When she succeeded she said she felt *'at ease; there was no more fear'*. For in saying 'Father, Son and Holy Spirit' she enters the Trinity, the community of love in whom there is no fear. For we who are Christians, the sign of the Cross is the greatest sign language we possess. When we make the sign of the Cross we know with whom we travel, whose word we can trust and share with others, and we know where we are going. We know the sign. Perhaps we just need to learn to speak the language in a better and deeper way.

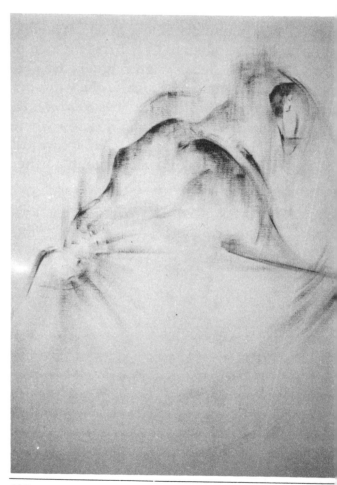

12. Springs of Living Water

For ten years I was Chaplain in Lourdes. I like to think of it as a 'decade' at the Grotto for Mary. It is part of my own personal rosary – part of the joyful, sorrowful and glorious mysteries that we experience on our own personal pilgrimage towards the heart of God. I cannot claim to have said the 'decade' well. That's for others and especially Another to decide. All I know is that it was a great mercy from God to have been able to have served so many pilgrims. And mercy is what Lourdes is all about.

Over these years I have often been asked why such a multitude of people come to Lourdes. It's not an easy question to answer. To have a more comprehensive response you would really need to ask each of the five million or so people who come every year to this Shrine. Even then you would probably have five million very different answers. Basically I think we come here because we are thirsty. There is an elemental thirst in the ch of us; a thirst for life, for answers to the yearnings of our hearts; a thirst for in body and in spirit; above all a thirst to love and be loved. Lourdes stands like an oasis in the wilderness of our times. It is a place where we can quench that thirst. *'Scrape away the soil and a spring will gush forth,'* Our Lady said to Bernadette. On one level she points to the physical; as Bernadette scrapes away the earth water comes forth. But on another level the Blessed Virgin points us beyond the physical to the spiritual. As we dig deeper we see that this is no mere water. It is the symbol of Jesus himself. He is the 'living water'.

We do not have to believe in apparitions, in any apparitions (although in the case of Lourdes I believe you would be a fool if you didn't). We are not obliged to, since they are not essential to our faith. What is so great about Lourdes is that it always brings us back to what is essential. The Blessed Virgin always points us in the direction of the Gospels. She always points us, under the guidance of the Holy Spirit, to Jesus her son who in turn reveals to us the Father's love. Lourdes is much more than processions and ceremonies. It is much more than a place of devotion. It is much more than a place of physical healing. It is about all a place in which we rediscover from the heart of God himself how much we are loved by him, how much we are held in his mercy.

In the Gospel story of the raising of Lazarus, two women, two sisters plead for the life of their dead brother. *'If only you had been here,'* they say to Jesus, *'this would not have happened.'* (Jn 11:21-23) It is the women who intercede in favour of life. It is the essence of a woman to give life. For a woman close to the cradle, the tomb is insufferable. Martha and Mary plead for Lazarus. They are on the side of life. In Lourdes another woman stands with us and for us on the side of life. It is the *'woman blessed amongst all women.'* Our Lady intercedes in favour of life, not one life, but the life of the whole of humanity. She is there with us in times of temptation to crush *'the head of the serpent'*. She is there in our times of difficulty when *the wine has run out'*. She stands at the foot of our every cross, praying and waiting for the victory of love. In naming herself here as the Immaculate Conception, Mary does more than remind us of her great priviledges before God. It is rather an affirmation that the purest of creatures stands with her children. Within the world of a child's heart, Mary comes to lead us back to the mystery of the Incarnation, to the Good News of the Gospels. She tells us clearly: Jesus is not absent. He is here, loving us, embracing us, *'with us always until the end of time.'* He is the *'Resurrection and the Life.'* He *'takes no pleasure in the death of the living.'* (Wis 1:13) His only concern is to raise us from the deadness that lies in our hearts and give us *'an abundance of life.'*

We still find it hard to believe we are lovable. With all the ugly things of our hearts, how can God possibly love us? But he does. That's the message of the Gospels. That's why Mary comes to a place that was a rubbish dump, a pig-sty, a place associated with the riff-raff of the times. She comes to such a place, not to deny our evil and our ugliness but so that we can learn to face it and transform it; to remind us we are the beloved of God and to enable us to rediscover the beauty of the image of God that is in us. That image cannot be destroyed. Even if it has been soiled, disfigured, tarnished, shattered by our sins and the sins of others, it is still there. Mary comes to call forth that better part of us and to lead us to the only one who can restore us to a greater likeness with his own heart. That's what Resurrection is about. Jesus who calls forth

Lazarus from the tomb. Jesus who calls forth each of us from what disfigures and deadens love and restores us again to the intimacy of love with the heavenly Father. '*As he was praying, the appearance of his face changed, and his clothes became dazzling white.*' (Lk 9:29) It is the account of the Transfiguration. We have a revelation of the intimacy Jesus shares with his Father. It is the revelation of what we are called to become, borne out by the presence of Moses and Elijah. It is a feast of human possibilities. We are meant to become radiant with the love of God. We are called to shine with an intimacy we have with the Lord. That's what happens to Bernadette, We are given two images. One, a child disfigured by the mud of the pig-sty. The other, a child who in ecstasy is '*more beautiful than Rachel (the star of the times) ever was at the height of her stardom.*' With Jesus we can move from disfigured hearts to transfigured hearts.

It is significant that the first person to whom Jesus appears after the Resurrection is Mary Magdalene. It is a confirmation of why he came into the world, '*to save the sick and the sinner.*' The Magdalene is just a poor sinner like we are. Touched by the love of Jesus, her life is made new and whole. It is transfigured and trans-

To heal a blind man Jesus takes the mud earth and puts it on his eyes. Using mud he s the miracle. We are the mud. We are the mud that Jesus wishes to transform. We are the mud to whom he opens the way for intimacy with the Father.

'We are an Easter people, and our song is alleluia,' said Pope John Paul II. Nowhere is that more evident than in Lourdes. There are people who come in sadness and despair. They often leave with new hope, new heart and new life. Here is a place where truly the 'blind see, the deaf hear, and the lame walk.' Not just in physical terms. But especially in the realm of the heart. 'Scrape away the soil and a spring will gush forth.' As we allow the mud of our lives to be washed away in the springs of God's mercy, we fulfill the dreams and desires God has for us.

Lourdes lies in a mountain valley. The surrounding countryside speaks of fresh pastures, of sheep and of shepherds. We are reminded of Bernadette, the little shepherdess. We are reminded of the words of the book of Revelation: 'He will be their shepherd and he will lead them to springs of living water.' (Rev 7:17)